The Giving Church

A 21-Day Prayer Journey Toward Generosity

David Butts

PRAYERSHOP
PUBLISHING

TERRE HAUTE, INDIANA

PrayerShop Publishing is the publishing arm of the Church Prayer Leaders Network. The Church Prayer Leaders Network exists to equip and inspire local churches and their prayer leaders in their desire to disciple their people in prayer and to become a "house of prayer for all nations." Its online store, prayershop.org, has more than 150 prayer resources available for purchase or download.

ISBN: 978-1-935012-90-0

1 2 3 4 5 | 2023 2022 2021 2020 2019

Contents

—

Introduction

This book can be helpful to anyone who wants to grow deeper in his or her giving life, but it particularly targets churches. From time to time, churches go through giving campaigns for various purposes, often related to paying off a mortgage or launching a building campaign. Sometimes it is a "catch-up" effort to remove debt and prepare a church for a new season. Or it may be a new missions focus. Some churches sponsor annual giving campaigns; others only on special occasions.

Whatever the reason for a financial initiative, it still comes down to individuals making decisions about what they will do with their finances. Each day of this devotional has a Scripture to shape your concepts of giving. Stories of generous churches and individuals are scattered throughout the book to offer encouragement as you give.

Ultimately, this devotional is intended to bring glory to Jesus. He is the Ultimate Giver. All that we own is a gift from Him. All that we give to Him will be used by Him to accomplish His purposes. Although this devotional focuses on giving, it's really about so much more! It's about receiving from the Lord and using it all in ways that bring Him honor and glory.

The Cries of Those in Need

Whoever closes his ear to the cry of the poor will himself call out and not be answered. (Proverbs 21:13)

The poor are everywhere and their needs can be overwhelming. Jesus said we would have the poor with us always (Mt. 26:11). Given this reality, how can a congregation meaningfully minister to the poor? We don't want to close our ears to their cries, but we need wisdom in how we attempt to meet the needs.

Given the astonishing array of ways we might minister to the poor, it is always right to begin in prayer. As we ask the Lord how best to open our ears to the cry of the poor, He will give direction in practical ways. Churches across the nation have discovered creative ways to use their resources to care for those who have very real needs.

A friend from the Dallas, Texas, area told me about a church that found a way to maximize finances in caring for others. Instead of devoting significant finances to commercial advertising, this Texas church decided to spend its money on something much more meaningful. On Easter Sunday, a pastor at the Covenant Church of Carrollton announced they had bought out and forgiven $100,000 worth of medical debt for local families. The church made the transaction through RIP Medical Debt—an American nonprofit that buys up and abolishes medical debt. Since medical debt can be bought by collection agencies for a fraction of what they're worth, $100,000 translates to more than $10 million in medical debt that has now been lifted off the shoulders of struggling Texas families. Imagine 4,229 families and veterans who received letters notifying them of forgiven medical debt because of this donation!

This is a church that did not close its ears to the cries of the poor. According to the Scripture passage, this act of generous giving actually opens the door for answered prayer. What begins with prayer for direction will lead to generosity, resulting in more answered prayer. A giving church will find itself walking in close intimacy with the Lord.

Prayer Points

- Ask the Lord how your church might reach the hurting in your area through creative, generous giving.
- Pray for a greater sensitivity for those who are poor.

My Prayer

Lord, You pour out Your blessings upon us in amazing ways. Thank You for being a generous God. Help us to reflect Your generosity in the ways we deal with others. We want to be a light in our community through our generosity.

Beyond Bargain Giving

Then Ornan said to David, "Take it, and let my lord the king do what seems good to him. See, I give the oxen for burnt offerings and the threshing sledges for the wood and the wheat for a grain offering; I give it all." But King David said to Ornan, "No, but I will buy them for the full price. I will not take for the LORD what is yours, nor offer burnt offerings that cost me nothing." (1 Chronicles 21:23-24)

I love a good deal. It's great when I can find what I'm looking for at half the regular price or less. Free is even better! But I have discovered that cheap or free is not always the best. Not only is there the issue of quality, but it may also change the way I view my purchase. Free doesn't seem as valuable. Cheap sometimes means I don't need to take care of the item like I would something expensive. Price affects perceived value.

King David understood this at a very basic level. When looking for a place to build the Temple, he was offered the ideal place for free. But he realized that price affects perceived value. How could he offer God a place for His sacred Temple that cost David nothing? Giving—especially extravagant, expensive giving—is an act of worship far beyond simply offering a free piece of property.

Our giving to God is not looking for the best bargain. It is not just trying to find the "biggest bang for our buck." It's hard to turn down a free piece of high-value property, especially when it looks like you're really getting a good Kingdom "deal."

What made David such a unique man of God was that he looked first to the value of the One receiving the gift. He realized he couldn't give a bargain gift to the King of the Universe.

The challenge for us is to look beyond the size of our capital campaign or budget initiative. Who is the real recipient of your gift? What do you want to give to the Savior of your soul? What kind of extravagant gift will you bring to your King?

Prayer Points

- Ask the Lord to help you overcome any sort of "bargain-giving" mentality.
- Pray for open eyes to see the majesty and awesomeness of the One to whom you are bringing your gifts.

My Prayer

Lord, You are an extravagant Giver to me. You have poured out physical and spiritual blessings upon me and I am grateful. Help me now to give back to You with that same kind of extravagance. May I, like David, not give to You what cost me nothing. Help me to see Your glory and respond appropriately with my giving.

Over-Abundant Giving

"Bezalel and Oholiab and every craftsman in whom the Lord has put skill and intelligence to know how to do any work in the construction of the sanctuary shall work in accordance with all that the Lord has commanded."

And Moses called Bezalel and Oholiab and every craftsman in whose mind the Lord had put skill, everyone whose heart stirred him up to come to do the work. And they received from Moses all the contribution that the people of Israel had brought for doing the work on the sanctuary. They still kept bringing him freewill offerings every morning, so that all the craftsmen who were doing every sort of task on the sanctuary came, each from the task that he was doing, and said to Moses, "The people bring much more than enough for doing the work that the Lord has commanded us to do." So Moses gave command, and word was proclaimed throughout the camp, "Let no man or woman do anything more for the contribution for the sanctuary." So the people were restrained from bringing, for the material they had was sufficient to do all the work, and more. (Exodus 36:1–7)

Imagine this common problem in churches everywhere: people giving too much! In this instance, Moses and the church leaders sent out an order to the whole congregation: "Quit giving! The abundance is starting to be a problem." Does this seem like a dream when you think of the Church today?

The story of over-abundant giving in Exodus 36 is not a dream. These were real people, just like us, who grasped a vision bigger than their own lives. They gave to the building of the Tabernacle, an ornate tent that preceded the building of the Temple and represented the Presence of God in their midst. This God-sized vision consumed them and caused them to give abundantly more than needed.

Could it be that our giving goals are too small with short-sighted vision? Of course, our building needs, our budget, and special projects are important. But is our call to give God-sized? Is there a promise of the Presence of God in our midst? Does it cause us to look for ways to give even more because we are so excited by the possibilities of God's work in our midst?

To have this big vision requires two things. First, it means church leadership couches any campaign in terms of spiritual victory and not just financial goals. Giving toward the Presence of God is a huge motivator for extravagant giving. The second requirement is for those of us in the congregation. We need to see with spiritual eyes what this campaign will accomplish in the Kingdom of God. Buildings aren't ultimately about brick and mortar. They are about ministry and changed lives. They are about places to worship and enjoy the Lord's Presence. They are tools in the hands of the Lord to accomplish His purpose.

Prayer Points

- Ask the Lord to give you the spiritual vision to see His purpose behind this campaign.
- Pray for a spirit of extravagant giving to be poured out on your congregation.

My Prayer

Lord, it is hard to imagine what happened in Moses' day when Your people gave so much that they were ordered to stop giving. Would You do that again in our day in our church? Give us a God-sized vision of what You want to do in our congregation. Give us an excitement about Your Kingdom and Your purposes that creates the kind of giving that we saw in Moses' day. We pray for abundance!

Dangerous Giving

Honor the LORD with your wealth and with the firstfruits of all your produce; then your barns will be filled with plenty, and your vats will be bursting with wine. (Proverbs 3:9–10)

This Scripture passage is dangerous. Although the biblical principle is absolutely true, it is risky. It can bring great harm if not used with understanding. Let me explain.

One clear way to honor the Lord is by giving back to Him. This includes making sure that the first use of your finances is directed toward honoring God. This is firstfruit giving. If the passage ended with this instruction, all would be fine.

But there's more. God promises an abundance given back to the giver. That's where the danger comes. Our motives can blur when the promise of abundance is made to firstfruit givers. This is when the condition of your heart is revealed. Are you giving to honor the Lord, or are you selfishly giving to receive back an abundance? Can you recognize the danger?

God's Word often connects abundant giving with abundant receiving. That's a good and godly principle. God delights in giving to us, especially when our giving habits demonstrate that money has no hold on us. When we honor God in our giving, we will continue to receive from Him, sometimes in physical or spiritual blessings.

It is a biblical principle that also tests our hearts. Why are we giving? If it is to honor God, then we are blessed. If we give simply to receive more, then money has attained mastery over us and we have failed the test. What is often called the prosperity gospel is false, mixed in with enough truth to make it dangerous. We do receive from God when we give. But God looks on the heart to determine our motives and real desires.

Let's decide today to give in a way that honors God. Put your giving *first* as you manage your budget. That's firstfruit giving! Then determine to give as an act of worship that doesn't look for anything other than the joy of giving. Guard your heart and expect God to work in you through your giving.

Prayer Points

- Ask the Lord to guard your heart regarding finances.
- Pray that God will show you what firstfruits giving looks like in your circumstance.

My Prayer

Lord, You are the Giver of every good and perfect gift. Thank You for the way You abundantly give to me. Help me to honor You with my wealth. Everything I have comes from You and I am grateful. Show me how to honor You in my giving and use of material blessings. Guard my heart, Lord, so that money does not grab hold of me and cause me to worship it. Show me the freedom in giving that releases Your power in my life.

Here's My Lunch

"There is a boy here who has five barley loaves and two fish, but what are they for so many?" (John 6:9)

It's a wonderful story of selfless giving. Five thousand hungry people and one little boy with his lunch. He gives it away with no thought of keeping anything for himself. Of course, we know the end of the story. Jesus takes the small gift in His hands and changes lives with it—something He still does today!

The town of West Union, Illinois, has a population of less than 300 people. The Christian Church there struggles to reach 100 in attendance on most Sundays. It's not a wealthy area with an abundance of resources, but the church always pays its bills. Beyond that is their Faith Promise, which is an annual commitment to missions that is above their regular church gift. For most, it is a faith stretch. In 2018, their Faith Promise giving was more than $70,000!

If you are in a larger church, a missions budget of $70,000 might not sound like much. But many churches larger than the West Union church don't give nearly as much to missions. You see, this small gift, given away to the larger Kingdom, is taken by the King and used to change lives.

Giving money away is not a burden but a privilege. God takes care of our needs. Although the text of John 6:9 doesn't tell us more specifics about the little boy, I believe he had plenty to eat that day. Jesus takes care of His generous followers.

What a privilege to give, whether as a little boy with fish and bread, or a congregation with a Kingdom vision. It isn't the size of the gift, but the hands of the King that make the difference.

Prayer Points

- Give thanks to the Lord for the privilege of giving.
- Ask the Lord to show you what sort of gift you can give that will make a difference in the hands of the King.

My Prayer

Lord, thank You for including in Scripture this story of the little boy who offered his lunch to You. We, too, are witnesses of this amazing miracle of provision. Thank You for giving us the same privilege—of placing in Your hands what You have already given to us. We want to keep our eyes open to see what You do with our gifts. Help us to be generous at all times!

No Strings Attached

But a man named Ananias, with his wife Sapphira, sold a piece of property, and with his wife's knowledge he kept back for himself some of the proceeds and brought only a part of it and laid it at the apostles' feet. But Peter said, "Ananias, why has Satan filled your heart to lie to the Holy Spirit and to keep back for yourself part of the proceeds of the land? While it remained unsold, did it not remain your own? And after it was sold, was it not at your disposal? Why is it that you have contrived this deed in your heart? You have not lied to man but to God." When Ananias heard these words, he fell down and breathed his last. And great fear came upon all who heard of it. The young men rose and wrapped him up and carried him out and buried him.

After an interval of about three hours his wife came in, not knowing what had happened. And Peter said to her, "Tell me whether you sold the land for so much." And she said, "Yes, for so much." But Peter said to her, "How is it that you have agreed together to test the Spirit of the Lord? Behold, the feet of those who have buried your husband are at the door, and they will carry you out." Immediately she fell down at his feet and breathed her last. When the young men came in they found her dead, and they carried her out and buried her beside her husband. And great fear came upon the whole church and upon all who heard of these things. (Acts 5:1–11)

Scary story, isn't it? We may not see the severe judgment of death in our churches today, but this scenario still happens. People fail to walk honestly before God and others. In this passage, money is at center stage. But Peter makes it clear that money is not the true issue. Ananias and Sapphira did not have to sell their property, and certainly did not have to give it all away. But they used money as a tool to deceive, and they paid the ultimate price for their deception.

There is still a tendency to use money—even money that we give or withhold—as a means of deception or manipulation. People might withhold money to show displeasure with a pastor or a project of a church. It has nothing to do with a question of biblical doctrine; it is simply because someone is unhappy about a person or direction. We need to examine our reason for giving. Are we giving to honor the Lord and advance His Kingdom or is it about manipulating our own way?

Money given to get one's way or to influence the direction of a church is money given wrongly. Peter said to Ananias, "While it remained unsold, did it not remain your own? And after it was sold, was it not at your disposal?" It really isn't about amounts, but about the heart. Can we give in a way that trusts the Lord to handle it, often through the spiritual leaders of the congregation? True giving means releasing money from our control and placing it under the Lord's control.

Jesus warned us about the power of money. It can control and distort our lives, even as well-intentioned followers of Jesus. Giving it away without trying to control or take credit is a wonderful, biblical way to break the power of money over our lives. As we live in this generous mode, the Lord will often provide even more for us to give away.

Prayer Points

- If money seems to be controlling too much of your thoughts and desires, confess that to the Lord and ask Him to show you how find freedom.
- Ask the Lord to give you a purity of heart regarding your giving.

My Prayer

Lord, thank You for providing for my every need. Because You are a Giver, You have made me like You. I want to give with no strings attached and no attempts to control the outcome. Forgive me when I try to manipulate people or situations with my money. Give me a purity of heart as I give generously to You.

Our Act of Worship

"But who am I, and what is my people, that we should be able thus to offer willingly? For all things come from you, and of your own have we given you. For we are strangers before you and sojourners, as all our fathers were. Our days on the earth are like a shadow, and there is no abiding. O LORD our God, all this abundance that we have provided for building you a house for your holy name comes from your hand and is all your own. I know, my God, that you test the heart and have pleasure in uprightness. In the uprightness of my heart I have freely offered all these things, and now I have seen your people, who are present here, offering freely and joyously to you." (1 Chronicles 29:14–17)

I am amazed at the clear insight God granted King David in so many areas, including giving and possessions. In his later years, David gathered everything needed for his son Solomon to build the Temple of God. David had insight to know that he needed to lead the way. He could not simply ask others to give. David freely outgave everyone! First Chronicles 29 lists the exact amounts. From a place of personal generosity, David challenged the nation to give.

And give they did! Both rich and poor gave in abundance and with great joy to build the House of God in Jerusalem. They did not give under compulsion or fear of David. According to David, generous giving tested their hearts spiritually and revealed "uprightness of heart" (vs. 17). The nation gave to God as an act of worship.

David acknowledged that everything they owned came from the hand of God. So few people today understand this, but David nailed it more than 3,000 years ago! It is this understanding of God as the Owner of all things that forms the basis for extraordinary giving.

David's principles are valid and effective for us today:

- Leaders must lead the way in generous giving.
- Giving tests our hearts and becomes an act of worship.
- Extraordinary giving comes from the realization that everything we have comes from God.

Prayer Points

- Ask the Lord to remind you often that everything you have comes from Him.
- Pray that God will make your giving an act of worship.

My Prayer

Lord, I believe with all my heart that everything I have comes from You. It is all Yours. Help me to live as a good steward of all that comes from Your hand. May my generous giving bring pleasure to You. I want to give joyously, as an act of worship and gratitude.

A Work of Grace

All the believers were one in heart and mind. No one claimed that any of their possessions was their own, but they shared everything they had. With great power the apostles continued to testify to the resurrection of the Lord Jesus. And God's grace was so powerfully at work in them all that there were no needy persons among them. For from time to time those who owned land or houses sold them, brought the money from the sales and put it at the apostles' feet, and it was distributed to anyone who had need. (Acts 4:32–35 NIV)

If there ever was a giving church, it was this first church in Jerusalem. Their newfound faith in Christ transformed every aspect of their lives, including how they viewed their possessions. These believers no longer tried to hold on to what they owned, but instead saw it as a way to meet the needs of others. The Lordship of Christ had meaning that moved from words to actions.

The phrase that jumps out is "there were no needy persons among them." This does not mean that people were neither rich nor poor; it's simply a way of life that says, "If I have something you need, I will freely give it to you." Instead of coercion or forced programs, this generosity was born out of hearts of compassion for others. And the result? No unmet needs among the believers!

Note something else that Acts 4 reveals about this generous church: "God's grace was so powerfully at work in them." God gifted them with a spirit of generosity because they understood everything belongs to God. When you truly believe this, you will eagerly share as the Lord directs. Generous giving becomes a work of grace in our lives.

If the Church today is to grow in extravagant giving, there must be a focus on God as Owner of everything. We are stewards of what already belongs to Him. God's grace is powerfully at work in us if we freely give like the early Jerusalem Church.

Prayer Points

- Ask the Lord to pour out a spirit of His grace upon your church.
- Pray that there will be no unmet needs in your congregation.

My Prayer

Lord, thank You for the wonderful example of a giving church in Acts 4. Help me reflect their same attitude of not claiming possessions as my own. Remind me that everything belongs to You. Show me how to meet the needs of others in godly ways. Please pour out Your grace upon my church so that we walk in generosity and abundance. We want to be a giving church like these brothers and sisters in Jerusalem.

Refreshing Others

A generous person will prosper; whoever refreshes others will be refreshed. (Proverbs 11:25 NIV)

Our God is a generous God. His followers will readily agree as they experience His generosity in physical, spiritual, and emotional ways. And because our Father wants His children to be like Him, His Word is filled with commands to be generous.

One common thread throughout these commands is reciprocity. If we are generous to others, we will receive increased generosity from God. Proverbs 11:25 promises that the generous person will prosper. This is a factual statement to be believed and acted upon, not debated. I love the way Christian pastor and author Mark Batterson explains it in *All In*:

> "I cannot prove this quantitatively, but I know it's true: the more you give away, the more you will enjoy what you have. If you give God the tithe, you'll enjoy the 90 percent you keep 10 percent more. You'll also discover that God can do more with 90 percent than you can do with 100 percent. . . . Most of us spend most of our lives accumulating the wrong things. We've bought into the consumerist lie that more is more. But in God's upside-down economy, our logic is backward. You ultimately lose whatever you keep and you ultimately keep whatever you lose for the cause of Christ."

I love the second phrase in Proverbs 11:25: "Whoever refreshes others will be refreshed." My wife Kim and I recently experienced this when her mom passed away and left a small inheritance. We chose to give away a portion to various ministries that we knew had needs. What a joy to write those checks! As we refreshed others financially, we experienced the same refreshing that God's Word promises.

Prayer Points

- Thank God for His amazing generosity to you.
- Ask the Lord to give you a spirit of generosity so that you might refresh others.

My Prayer

Lord, I am in awe of Your continuing generosity to me. In every way, You have blessed me—and I am grateful. I want the same giving spirit to characterize my life. Show me how to build generosity into everyday living. Lead me by Your Spirit to refresh others in generous ways.

Transforming Presence of Christ

He entered Jericho and was passing through. And behold, there was a man named Zacchaeus. He was a chief tax collector and was rich. And he was seeking to see who Jesus was, but on account of the crowd he could not, because he was small in stature. So he ran on ahead and climbed up into a sycamore tree to see him, for he was about to pass that way. And when Jesus came to the place, he looked up and said to him, "Zacchaeus, hurry and come down, for I must stay at your house today." So he hurried and came down and received him joyfully. And when they saw it, they all grumbled, "He has gone in to be the guest of a man who is a sinner." And Zacchaeus stood and said to the Lord, "Behold, Lord, the half of my goods I give to the poor. And if I have defrauded anyone of anything, I restore it fourfold." And Jesus said to him, "Today salvation has come to this house, since he also is a son of Abraham. For the Son of Man came to seek and to save the lost." (Luke 19:1–10)

There is something about the Presence of Jesus that changes everything. The little bit of time Zacchaeus spent with Jesus changed his whole life. It turned him from a selfish, corrupt tax collector, obsessed with money, into a generous follower of Jesus, who gave away his wealth. He was transformed by Jesus at the place of his greatest weakness—his love of money.

We all need the transforming touch of Jesus' hand. In our Western culture, the love of money can shape the direction of our lives. Choices of college, careers, and even family decisions are often made with an eye toward financial success. Biblically speaking, making money is never considered the problem. The issue is how we use money or allow it to control us.

That's why the Presence of Jesus is so important. He straightens out wrong priorities and sets us on a right path under His control. Of course, His most important role is forgiving us, bringing us into His family, and wrapping His loving arms around us. That's what Zacchaeus really needed. As a tax collector he was despised and shunned. Jesus faced criticism just for deciding to go to his house. But the Son of Man was not deterred from His ultimate mission.

It is fascinating that there is no indication Jesus spoke to Zacchaeus about his money. Yet this new convert announced publicly he would give away half of all he owned, as well as return four times the amount he defrauded from people.

Such is the transforming Presence of Jesus. As you move through a financial campaign, focus more on the Presence of Christ in you than on amounts of money to be raised. The Presence of Jesus offers a freedom in giving that is astonishing in its abundance.

Prayer Points

- Ask the Lord to show you the extent that money might have an unhealthy hold on your life.
- Pray that you will experience the Presence of Jesus in a life-transforming way.

My Prayer

Lord, I so long to dwell in Your Presence. Wake me up to who You are and Your life in me. I ask You to transform me in every way. Like Zacchaeus, I don't want money or anything else to create a barrier in following You. Give me a generous spirit that breaks any unhealthy hold money might have on me.

Give It All

Jesus looked up and saw the rich putting their gifts into the offering box, and he saw a poor widow put in two small copper coins. And he said, "Truly, I tell you, this poor widow has put in more than all of them. For they all contributed out of their abundance, but she out of her poverty put in all she had to live on." (Luke 21:1–4)

It's exciting when, in the middle of a building campaign, the Spirit moves on someone to give a huge gift. There's a buzz in our meetings, creating a sense of "we can do this" among the congregation. Large and unexpected gifts can make a difference!

But what is the response of heaven to big gifts? I believe there is joy over a generous gift given for right reasons. But I also think this rejoicing is a bit muted compared to the smaller, sacrificial gift given by the widow, the child, or the older couple on a fixed income. That's party time in heaven! God is looking for those who give with sacrifice.

Churches that launch financial campaigns often speak of equal giving, meaning not equal amounts but equal sacrifice. That's hard for the wealthy! They establish comfortable lifestyles while giving away generous amounts, but that is not equal to giving everything away. Equal sacrifice is not an easy thing to do. Jesus points toward this kind of giving in this well-known story of the widow's sacrifice.

What if Jesus is calling you to give it all away? I'm not saying He is, but *what if?* There's a good chance that those who have much can give it all away—and more will come within a few weeks. A lifetime of living with good financial principles ensures that finances will still flow. Are you willing to join with the widow and receive the blessing of a generous giver?

Prayer Points

- Ask the Lord to show you what you are to give.
- Pray for the ability to lay down your sense of ownership.

My Prayer

Lord, I'm so grateful for all the abundance You have given to me. Help me now to give it back with no regrets. Give me the heart of a giver. May I give it all away, trusting You to continue to provide.

More Than Writing a Check

Jesus replied, "A man was going down from Jerusalem to Jericho, and he fell among robbers, who stripped him and beat him and departed, leaving him half dead. Now by chance a priest was going down that road, and when he saw him he passed by on the other side. So likewise a Levite, when he came to the place and saw him, passed by on the other side. But a Samaritan, as he journeyed, came to where he was, and when he saw him, he had compassion. He went to him and bound up his wounds, pouring on oil and wine. Then he set him on his own animal and brought him to an inn and took care of him. And the next day he took out two denarii and gave them to the innkeeper, saying, 'Take care of him, and whatever more you spend, I will repay you when I come back.' Which of these three, do you think, proved to be a neighbor to the man who fell among the robbers?" He said, "The one who showed him mercy." And Jesus said to him, "You go, and do likewise." (Luke 10:30–37)

G iving often means money. But sometimes it is more than that. Jesus' classic story of the Good Samaritan certainly goes beyond giving money to demonstrating true compassion. This Samaritan, hated by all, reaches out with love, binds up a hurting man's wounds, and takes him to an inn where he can continue to heal. He leaves money to take care of the injured man's needs, but offers to give more the next time he comes by.

This doesn't mean our job is to be on the lookout for someone who has been beaten so that we can come to the rescue. It does mean we give in more ways than writing a check. Generosity can often be linked with hospitality. Are there ways we can open our homes to those with needs?

My home congregation, the Maryland Community Church in Terre Haute, Indiana, has a huge emphasis on foster care. What an amazing way to bring the hurting into your home and minister to them at a crucial time in their lives! Groups form alongside foster care families to help provide meals, offer respite care, and give encouragement. It's a great example of giving more than a check.

Regular giving forms a basis for the giving lifestyle. Sometimes, like in the story of the Good Samaritan, an opportunity presents itself to go beyond financial giving. Volunteering in a cause that you care about brings it full circle.

Prayer Points

- Ask the Lord to give you open eyes to see the needs of those around you.
- Ask God to show you how to give in a way that meets needs beyond writing a check.

My Prayer

Lord, Your life is a story of giving and meeting needs. Help me to be like You. Increase my awareness of the needs of those around me. Give me the ability to pour my life into the hurting. I want to be generous with both my giving and my life.

Opened Doors to Healing

After he had finished all his sayings in the hearing of the people, he entered Capernaum. Now a centurion had a servant who was sick and at the point of death, who was highly valued by him. When the centurion heard about Jesus, he sent to him elders of the Jews, asking him to come and heal his servant. And when they came to Jesus, they pleaded with him earnestly, saying, "He is worthy to have you do this for him, for he loves our nation, and he is the one who built us our synagogue." And Jesus went with them. When he was not far from the house, the centurion sent friends, saying to him, "Lord, do not trouble yourself, for I am not worthy to have you come under my roof. Therefore I did not presume to come to you. But say the word, and let my servant be healed. For I too am a man set under authority, with soldiers under me: and I say to one, 'Go,' and he goes; and to another, 'Come,' and he comes; and to my servant, 'Do this,' and he does it." When Jesus heard these things, he marveled at him, and turning to the crowd that followed him, said, "I tell you, not even in Israel have I found such faith." And when those who had been sent returned to the house, they found the servant well. (Luke 7:1–10)

A side from being a man of great faith, we don't know much about this Roman centurion. Separated from family and friends, he made the best of things in a strange land. He came to love the Jewish people and even built them a synagogue. Perhaps he gave money or sent men from his troops to help. Whatever the cost, it certainly wasn't cheap! His generosity reaped the undying love and respect of the Jewish leaders in Capernaum.

We need to keep watch for opportunities to give to those who are different from us. Imagine the differences between this pagan Roman officer and the strict Jews who were under his control. In some situations, the Jews looked for ways to kill the Romans who were dominating their lives—and in response, the Romans were often cruel and domineering. But not in Capernaum. The act of giving to build a place of worship and learning for the Jews opened the door for good relationships.

Our giving becomes a tool in the hands of the Lord to build relationships and advance His Kingdom. It isn't just about the money. It is about demonstrating love and commitment to Jesus. Given properly, it invites the Presence of Christ in ways that bring healing.

I don't believe the Roman centurion understood this when he built the Jewish synagogue in Capernaum. But his giving opened doors and restored relationships. And when his servant's need came along, it brought the healing Presence of Christ to his household.

Just imagine what might happen in our lives when we give generously toward the cause of Christ.

Prayer Points

- Ask the Lord to make you aware of the needs of those who are different from you.
- Pray for the Presence of Christ to be present in your giving campaign.

My Prayer

Lord, what a wonderful story of generosity and healing in Capernaum! I want to see that happen in my city as well. Pour out a spirit of generosity. Help me to give, even to those who are different from me. Please use my giving to build relationships and bridges—and to accomplish Your purposes.

First to the Lord

We want you to know, brothers, about the grace of God that has been given among the churches of Macedonia, for in a severe test of affliction, their abundance of joy and their extreme poverty have overflowed in a wealth of generosity on their part. For they gave according to their means, as I can testify, and beyond their means, of their own accord, begging us earnestly for the favor of taking part in the relief of the saints—and this, not as we expected, but they gave themselves first to the Lord and then by the will of God to us. Accordingly, we urged Titus that as he had started, so he should complete among you this act of grace. But as you excel in everything—in faith, in speech, in knowledge, in all earnestness, and in our love for you—see that you excel in this act of grace also. (2 Corinthians 8:1–7)

It's dangerous to give on your own. It can easily become a way of control or manipulation—or even an attempt to buy into the Kingdom. The Macedonians had no such problem. Their giving began with God first extending His grace to them. And with His grace, came a spirit of giving that has astonished Christ-followers for 2,000 years.

The Macedonian church was not a wealthy church by any means. But God poured out His grace upon the three factors of their church life: severe affliction, abundance of joy, and extreme poverty. The result was an overflowing in the wealth of generosity! They gave according to their means, and, as Paul put it, even beyond their means. They pleaded with Paul to allow them to help the starving Christians in Judea, providing out of their poverty in an astonishing way.

Paul was amazed that they got it right. They gave themselves first to the Lord and then to Paul. That's always the first step in abundant giving—offering yourself to the Lord! All we have comes from the Lord, and sometimes He asks for it back. That's when our giving reflects great joy, realizing the privilege to give back to the Lord as He directs.

Our giving today isn't for starving Christians in Judea. But we must still follow the Macedonian believers' example. We give ourselves first to the Lord and then to those who are in spiritual leadership over us. This, combined with the grace of God, will result in an outpouring of the wealth of generosity.

Prayer Points

- Ask the Lord to make you aware of the gift of His grace to your congregation.
- Offer yourself and your family to the Lord.

My Prayer

Lord, You are the Giver of every good and perfect gift. Thank You! Please pour out Your grace upon my church in obvious and special ways. Lord, we offer ourselves back to You. All that we have and all that we are comes from You. Lord, take anything and everything that is needed. We give it to You!

Deposits into Your Heavenly Account

As for the rich in this present age, charge them not to be haughty, nor to set their hopes on the uncertainty of riches, but on God, who richly provides us with everything to enjoy. They are to do good, to be rich in good works, to be generous and ready to share, thus storing up treasure for themselves as a good foundation for the future, so that they may take hold of that which is truly life. (1 Timothy 6:17–18)

Most of the early believers were poor, but not all. A small segment of the early Church was made up of business people and the wealthy. Paul gives clear commands regarding their use of wealth. In today's culture, almost without exception, everyone reading this book fits the criteria of the wealthy. In other words, these commands are for you, too.

The first area of command is not to trust in your wealth, but in God. He is the Provider of all you have. It's harder for the wealthy to accept this truth because many worked hard for their wealth. Others grew up with it. Either way, wealth is a significant part of their lives and it is hard not to trust in those resources.

But here is how to avoid trusting in wealth:

1. Do good.
2. Be rich in good deeds.
3. Be generous.
4. Be willing to share.

In other words, be ready to give your money away where it is needed. Wealthy believers must look for ways to make a difference with what God has entrusted to them. That's how they proclaim their trust in the Lord.

Paul says that if the wealthy do those things, they will lay up treasure for themselves. It reflects the Lord's command to store treasures in heaven rather than on earth (Mt. 6:19–21). Treasures in heaven come from activities on earth. When we give generously on earth, our account in heaven will grow.

I have several accounts in my bank. When I am paid, I take time to move the money around to different accounts. It's still my money, but it is in different accounts. In a very real sense, this is what you are doing when you give generously. It goes to an account with your name on it in heaven. It's safe there!

Money in your heavenly account provides a solid foundation for your eternal life. It isn't buying your way into heaven—you can't do that! But it is a way we lay up treasure eternally. We grab hold of the life that is truly life. Your money here is subject to the ups and downs of the market or similar convulsions. But your money in heaven changes things on earth that in turn changes things in heaven.

Prayer Points

- Ask the Lord to give you a firm understanding of how He provides everything we need.
- Pray God will show you how to be rich in good deeds.

My Prayer

Lord, I am so grateful that everything I have comes from You. Please show me how to be rich in good deeds. I want to be generous and give without hesitation as You lead. I know my treasure is in heaven. May whatever I give on earth be posted to my account in heaven, providing a firm foundation for life eternal.

Learn to Excel at Giving

The point is this: whoever sows sparingly will also reap sparingly, and whoever sows bountifully will also reap bountifully. Each one must give as he has decided in his heart, not reluctantly or under compulsion, for God loves a cheerful giver. And God is able to make all grace abound to you, so that having all sufficiency in all things at all times, you may abound in every good work. As it is written,

"He has distributed freely, he has given to the poor; his righteousness endures forever."

He who supplies seed to the sower and bread for food will supply and multiply your seed for sowing and increase the harvest of your righteousness. You will be enriched in every way to be generous in every way, which through us will produce thanksgiving to God. For the ministry of this service is not only supplying the needs of the saints but is also overflowing in many thanksgivings to God. By their approval of this service, they will glorify God because of your submission that comes from your confession of the gospel of Christ, and the generosity of your contribution for them and for all others, while they long for you and pray for you, because of the surpassing grace of God upon you. Thanks be to God for his inexpressible gift! (2 Corinthians 9:6–15)

In *The Treasure Principle*, Randy Alcorn shares the story of Scott Lewis, owner of Scott Machinery, who attended a conference where Bill Bright challenged people to give one million dollars to help fulfill the Great Commission. This amount was laughable to Scott—far beyond anything he could imagine, since his machinery business was generating an income of under $50,000 a year.

Bill asked, "How much did you give last year?" Scott felt good about his answer: "We gave $17,000, about 35 percent of our income." Without blinking an eye, Bill responded, "Over the next year, why don't you make a goal of giving $50,000?"

Scott thought Bill hadn't understood. Fifty thousand dollars was more than he'd made all year! But Scott and his wife decided to trust God with Bill's challenge, asking Him to do the impossible. God provided in amazing ways. Because of a miraculous December 31 provision, the Lewises gave the $50,000. The next year they set a goal of giving $100,000. Again, God provided.

Scott wrote Alcorn a note saying that they passed the one million-dollar giving mark in 2001. The best part is they aren't stopping. That's what it means to excel at giving.

Paul declares in this passage, "You will be enriched in every way to be generous in every way" (vs. 11). The story of the Lewis family is a good example of this spiritual principle. Start with what you have and ask the Lord to bless it for the purpose of making you more generous. Take Him up on His offer. Watch and see what He does as you stretch yourself to give beyond your means.

Then note the result of this—to produce thanksgiving to God. He receives the praise and thanks because it is obvious to all that this abundance comes from His hand. We don't give to be recognized; we give *so that God is recognized*. He receives the glory for the wonder of His inexpressible gift to us!

Prayer Points

- Ask the Lord for a giving goal that is beyond your ability, but not His.
- Thank the Lord for His inexpressible gift!

My Prayer

Lord, You are the majestic Giver of all that I have. I bow before You in gratitude for Your amazing gifts. Will You help me to pass along Your blessings to others? Show me how to give in a way that brings fresh thanksgiving to You. Stretch my giving to look more like the giving of my Lord.

Except You Only

And you Philippians yourselves know that in the beginning of the gospel, when I left Macedonia, no church entered into partnership with me in giving and receiving, except you only. Even in Thessalonica you sent me help for my needs once and again. (Philippians 4:15–16)

It's nice to be a part of a group that is giving toward a common goal. You can get excited by watching how others are giving and by the steadily growing amount of funds as you edge closer to your goal. The giving of others brings you encouragement as you mature in your own stewardship.

But what if you are the only one giving toward a cause? That's when you need to focus on the Giver of every good and perfect gift to help sustain your giving. It's what happened with the Philippians. They gave to Paul while he was with them, and then continued to give even after he left. They believed in his mission and knew he needed their help. They built a relationship with him and marked it through their regular gifts.

Sometimes God puts you in a position like the Philippians. You see a need and stick with it. God honors that sort of quiet giving. Paul needed the faithfulness of the Philippians. He said of them, "no church entered in partnership with me in giving and receiving, except you only."

Pay attention to the needs around you, especially the mission needs of those who might not attract much attention from others. Perhaps it's the new church plant in your area that seems to be gasping for breath financially. As God leads you into these areas of giving, do it quietly, even if it's "except you only." When you honor God, He will bless you!

Prayer Points

- Ask the Lord if there is someone you need to bless with your giving.
- Thank the Lord for giving you the resources to help others.

My Prayer

Lord, I am so grateful that You have blessed me with the resources I need to bless others. What a privilege to pass along Your blessings. Help me to keep my spiritual eyes and ears open to discern how You might be leading me to give. Give me the wisdom to give without needing recognition or appreciation.

Test Me in This

"Bring the whole tithe into the storehouse, that there may be food in my house. Test me in this," says the Lord Almighty, "and see if I will not throw open the floodgates of heaven and pour out so much blessing that there will not be room enough to store it." (Malachi 3:10, NIV)

Few things prompt as much debate as the issue of tithing. Should the Christian today tithe? Is the ten percent a requirement? One thing I've noticed in this discussion: those who support tithing, tithe. Those who do not support tithing, do not tithe. It seems we have reduced the conversation to personal preferences. I think we can do better than this.

The passage from Malachi is, in a sense, a challenge from God regarding tithing. "Test me in this," with tithing being "this." In Old Testament times, the tithe was clearly in force and yet people still struggled against it. God put down this gauntlet, challenging the people to give the whole tithe and then watch how He would respond. He promised that tithe given freely opens the floodgates of heaven and pours out great blessing.

We can argue about the tithe being in force today or not, but the real issue is that this challenge from the Lord is certainly still active. Who would not want to receive blessing from above in such measure that there is not enough room to store it? Would we not want to see our tithes open the floodgates of heaven?

My friend Barry Cameron says that the tithe is not the finishing line but the starting line for the Christian. I think that's a great way of looking at it. Start at ten percent and then begin to increase that percentage through the years and watch how the Lord blesses. God invites you to test Him!

Prayer Points

- Ask the Lord about tithing—and then listen carefully with your heart.
- Pray about where you should direct your tithe, recognizing the local church is typically the recipient.

My Prayer

Lord, thank You for Your generosity! I am so grateful. Thank You for this challenge to tithe. I want this to be a good beginning place for me as I learn to give back to You. May I continue to grow in giving way beyond the tithe. Help me to keep my eyes on You as I watch how You open the storehouse of heaven in response to my tithe.

Hilarious Giving

Each one must give as he has decided in his heart, not reluctantly or under compulsion, for God loves a cheerful giver. (2 Corinthians 9:7)

Some translators point out that the word we translate here as "cheerful" often means "hilarious." I love that God loves a hilarious giver. It's someone so overcome with the delight of giving that they laugh in their generosity. In my mom's family, when we start laughing, it often brings tears to our eyes. We call them Crumrin tears (my mom's maiden name). Don't you love the picture of someone laughing to the point of tears as they write out a check?

That might be carrying it a bit far, but it really is the perspective on giving from heaven's viewpoint. It's the believer who has decided, under the direction of the Spirit, to give a great amount for a cause. It becomes a hilarious action. It's more than they can afford and doesn't make sense financially. But since it's all God's anyway, let's write the check and laugh. Maybe even laugh until we cry!

The Easter Seals Rehabilitation Center in Evansville, Indiana, excitedly anticipates a call from an old friend during the month between Thanksgiving and Christmas. Last year Terry Haynie, vice president of development, answered the call on a typical workday on November 30. "Do you know what time of year it is?" a mischievous-sounding male voice asked. This question signals the start of a mysterious annual treasure hunt. "Yes, sir," Haynie replied. "It's Pete's time!"

Every year the caller, who identifies himself only as Pete, phones the center with a clue-filled message that sends the staff on a search of the two-story building and its grounds to find Pete's donation to children with disabilities. In the past, this "Secret Santa" has stashed money in a snowman cookie jar and attached it to candy canes hung from a tree by the parking lot. More recently, his instructions led staff members out the door, around to the back of the building, and toward a dumpster. There they found a gift bag containing a miniature tin Christmas tree dangling 30 crisp $100 bills from its branches. At the sight of the treasure, the staff members always applaud, wave, and yell, "Thank you, Pete!" with the hope he is watching.

Since 1990, Pete has donated nearly $65,000 to the center, which serves 5,000 adults and children in need of physical and medical rehabilitation in a 30-county stretch of Indiana, Illinois, and Kentucky. Pete asks only that his gifts help the children served by the center. "He always says to use his gifts to make Christmas merrier for the kids whose families can't afford it," Haynie reports. Last year, 70 children got new clothes and toys because of Pete. And every year, his donation comes with a note on purple paper that promises, "You will hear from me again!" That's hilarious giving—and God loves it!

Prayer Points

- Ask the Lord to make you a cheerful giver.
- Pray that the Lord will make it clear how you are to give, even to the exact amounts.

My Prayer

Lord, how delightful it is to give as You give. Please make me a cheerful giver, a hilarious giver. I want to laugh as I write checks bigger than I should be able to write. I thank You for not pressing in on me through compulsion or guilt. You have set me free to give in a way that blesses others and honors Your name.

Rich in Every Way

For you know the grace of our Lord Jesus Christ, that though he was rich, yet for your sake he became poor, so that you through his poverty might become rich. (2 Corinthians 8:9)

Eddie Ogan is a grandmother from Colville, Washington. She wrote in a denominational newsletter about an experience when she was 14 years old as she and two sisters were living with their widowed mom in 1946:

"A month before Easter, the pastor of our church announced that a special Easter offering would be taken to help a poor family. He asked everyone to save and give sacrificially. When we got home, we talked about what we could do. We decided to buy 50 pounds of potatoes and live on them for a month. This would allow us to save $20 of our grocery money for the offering.

"Then we thought that if we kept our electric lights turned out as much as possible and didn't listen to the radio, we'd save money on that month's electric bill. [My sister] Darlene got as many house and yard cleaning jobs as possible, and both of us babysat for everyone we could. . . .

"That month was one of the best of our lives. Every day we counted the money to see how much we had saved. . . . Every Sunday the pastor had reminded everyone to save for the sacrificial offering. The day before Easter, [my sister] Ocy and I walked to the grocery store and got the manager to give us three crisp $20 bills and one $10 bill for all our change. . . . We could hardly wait to get to church!

"When the sacrificial offering was taken, we were sitting on the second row from the front. Mom put in the $10 bill, and each of us girls put in a $20. As we walked home after church, we sang all the way. At lunch Mom had a surprise for us. She had bought a dozen eggs, and we had boiled Easter eggs with our fried potatoes!

"Late that afternoon the minister drove up in his car. Mom went to the door, talked with him for a moment, and then came back with an envelope in her hand. We asked what it was, but she didn't say a word. She opened the envelope and out fell a bunch of money. There were three crisp $20 bills, one $10 bill and seventeen $1 bills.

Mom put the money back in the envelope. We didn't talk, just sat and stared at the floor. We had gone from feeling like millionaires to feeling [poor].

". . . All that week, we girls went to school and came home, and no one talked much. Finally on Saturday, Mom asked us what we wanted to do with the money. What did poor people do with money? We didn't know. We'd never known we were poor.

". . . At church [that Sunday] we had a missionary speaker. He talked about how churches in Africa made buildings out of sun-dried bricks, but they need money to buy roofs. He said $100 would put a roof on a church. The minister said, 'Can't we all sacrifice to help these poor people?'

"We looked at each other and smiled for the first time in a week. Mom reached into her purse and pulled out the envelope. She passed it to Darlene. Darlene gave it to me, and I handed it to Ocy. Ocy put it in the offering plate. When the offering was counted, the minister announced that it was a little over $100. The missionary was excited. He hadn't expected such a large offering from our small church. He said, 'You must have some rich people in this church.'

"Suddenly it struck us! We had given $87 of that 'little over $100.' We were the rich family in the church! Hadn't the missionary said so? From that day on I've never been poor again."

—Story is taken from "The Rich Family in Our Church" (bible.org/rich-family-our-church)

It's a powerful story of being poor, yet having everything. Giving changes your perspective on life. This dear family followed in the steps of their Lord Jesus by giving sacrificially toward the needs of others. In the process, they became rich in every way.

Prayer Points

- Ask the Lord to help you experience the grace of Jesus every day.
- Pray that the Lord will show you how to be rich by embracing the poverty of Jesus.

My Prayer

Lord, You have poured Your grace out upon us. Thank You! Show us, please, how You laid aside the riches of heaven for the poverty of life on earth. We lay down our wealth before You and embrace Your poverty. We know Lord, in doing this, we will again be made rich by You.

Unusual Means

Soon afterward he went on through cities and villages, proclaiming and bringing the good news of the kingdom of God. And the twelve were with him, and also some women who had been healed of evil spirits and infirmities: Mary, called Magdalene, from whom seven demons had gone out, and Joanna, the wife of Chuza, Herod's household manager, and Susanna, and many others, who provided for them out of their means. (Luke 8:1–3)

It was a most unusual means of funding a ministry. Some women who had been healed of infirmities and demon possession were following Jesus and His friends, and were paying for their needs. Most of us would avoid that sort of association. But Jesus saw beyond their past. He used their gifts with joy.

He still uses unusual means to fund ministries. John Bechtel, a missionary in Hong Kong, wanted to start a Christian camp to reach people for Christ. A bankrupt multimillion-dollar hotel and conference center became available for sale. He made an offer to purchase the property and then traveled around the world to raise the millions he would need. But no one was willing to help, so he returned to Hong Kong discouraged. Then he received a letter from a young girl that included $1 and a note saying she wanted him to use it to buy the camp. Bechtel prayed and took the girl's $1 to the real estate closing. The corporation decided to accept the $1 as full payment! Since the camp first opened, more than a million people have attended and more than 100,000 have accepted Christ.

A $1 gift from a young girl has been multiplied many times over and is a major tool in the Lord's hands to bring people to Himself. What do you think He might do with your gift? You might not have much to give, but when given in the right spirit and with a desire to serve the Lord, it becomes huge in the eyes of the Lord. He takes what we have and multiplies it in significant ways.

Jesus took the gifts given by these women and used them to provide for His disciples and His own needs. Some of these women did not have the best reputations. That didn't matter to Jesus. He knew their hearts. He had poured His life into them and they would never be the same. Their gifts were sanctified by His Presence and used for His purpose. So, too, will your gifts be used by the Lord to advance His Kingdom and accomplish His desires.

Prayer Points

- Ask the Lord to allow you to lay what you have at His feet.
- Pray that the Lord will use your gifts to advance His Kingdom.

My Prayer

Lord Jesus, I love You! I am so grateful that You allow me to give in a way that brings blessing to You. I want Your Kingdom to grow and Your purposes to be accomplished. Take what I have and use it however You desire. Bring glory and honor to Yourself through my gifts to You.

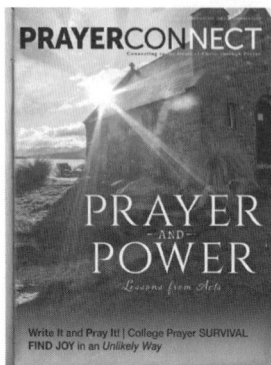

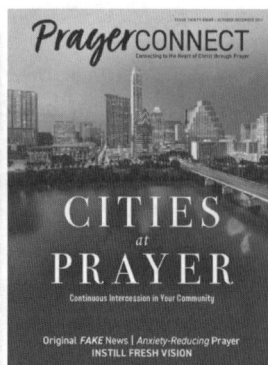